CLIMATE

Torrey Maloof

Consultant

Catherine Hollinger, CID, CLIA
EPA WaterSense Partner
Environmental Consultant

Image Credits: Cover, p.1 iStock; p.22 (top)
Cornforth Images/Alamy; p.15 (bottom) Dennis Cox/
Alamy; p.15 (top) imageBROKER/Alamy; p.11 (top)
Juniors Bildarchiv GmbH/Alamy; p.20 (top) Stock
Connection Blue/Alamy; p.25 (illustrations) Tim
Bradley; p.27 (top) Anna Henly/Getty Images;
p.24 (top) Flip Nicklin/Minden Pictures/Getty
Images; backcover, pp. 4–11 (background), 13 (top),
14–15 (background), 22–23 (background), 25, 30–31
iStock; p.19 (top) NOAA; pp.28–29 (illustrations)
Janelle Bell-Martin; pp.5, 11 (bottom) Courtney
Patterson; p.7 (bottom) Gary Hincks/Science Source;
all other images from Shutterstock.

Library of Congress Cataloging-in-Publication Data

Maloof, Torrey, author.
  Climate / Torrey Maloof.
    pages cm
  Summary: "If you travel far away, how do you know
what type of clothes to pack? You don't want to bring
sandals if it's snowing! You need to know what the
climate is. Different areas have different climates.
Learning about the climates of different places will
prepare you for any kind of weather"—Provided by
publisher.
  Audience: K to grade 3.
  Includes index.
  ISBN 978-1-4807-4649-7 (pbk.)
  ISBN 1-4807-4649-5 (pbk.)
  ISBN 978-1-4807-5093-7 (ebook)
1. Climatology—Juvenile literature.
2. Climatic zones—Juvenile literature.
3. Climatic changes—Juvenile literature. I. Title.
  QC863.5.M35 2015
  551.6—dc23
                                    2014034279

Teacher Created Materials
5301 Oceanus Drive
Huntington Beach, CA 92649-1030
http://www.tcmpub.com
ISBN 978-1-4807-4649-7

Table of Contents

Weather Versus Climate

What clothes will you wear tomorrow? Will you bundle up in a scarf and a sweater? Or, will you wear shorts and sandals? Weather determines the clothes you wear on any given day. Weather is the state of the air outside at a certain time and place. But what if you want to predict what you'll be wearing in the next few months? You'll want to know what time of year it will be. And you'll want to know where you will be. Climate is the weather pattern found in a specific place over many years.

Check out how weather in the past can help predict future climate changes by visiting http://www.oldweather.org.

Climate affects the health of people, plants, and animals. It even affects the quality of the soil, the air, and the water. If we want to know what the climate will be like in the future, we need to understand what causes changes in the climate. Scientists often compare Earth's climate to the past. This helps them understand how the climate is changing. And it helps them predict the changes that might occur in the future.

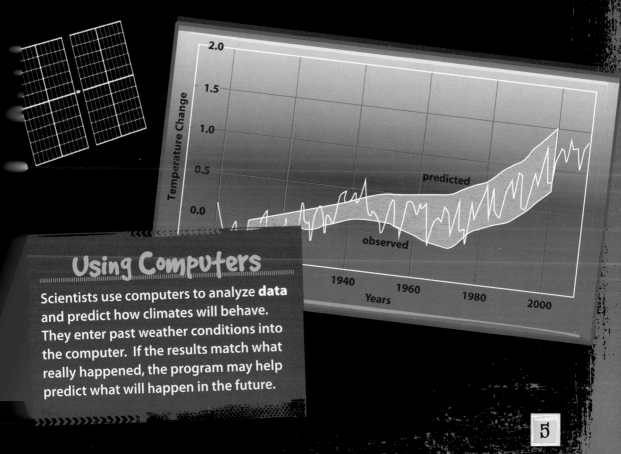

Using Computers

Scientists use computers to analyze **data** and predict how climates will behave. They enter past weather conditions into the computer. If the results match what really happened, the program may help predict what will happen in the future.

Many things play a role in climate. Wind has a big job. The direction it blows and the amount of **moisture** it brings affect climate. Little wind with low moisture makes for a dry climate.

Mountains influence climate, too. They force the air to rise. This creates moisture. Resulting in a wet climate on one side of the mountain. But it creates a dry climate on the other side of the mountain.

The world's oceans impact climate, as well. They add moisture to the air. Oceans can also absorb and store heat from the sun. This affects air temperature.

Scientists take into account all these factors and more when describing an area's climate. They analyze the weather data. They look at the amount of rain and snow. They also look closely at the plants that live in an area. Plants can tell scientists a lot about climate. So can the local animals.

Rain Shadow

A rain shadow is a patch of land that has become a desert because mountains block rainy weather. As air rises up the side of a mountain, moisture is squeezed out. When the air falls on the other side, it is dry.

Climate Zones

The world is divided into different climate zones, or areas. There are three main groups of climates: low-latitude climates, mid-latitude climates, and high-latitude climates. These groups are named for their closeness to the **equator**.

Low-latitude climates are closest to the equator. They are tropical. This means they tend to be very warm.

Mid-latitude climates are farther away from the equator. They are temperate. This means they are not too cold or too hot. These are **mild** climates.

High-latitude climates are the farthest from the equator. They are polar, or arctic, regions. This means they are very cold. This group includes the North and South Poles and other frosty locations.

Within each of these groups are little groups of climates. Let's look at these climate zones more closely.

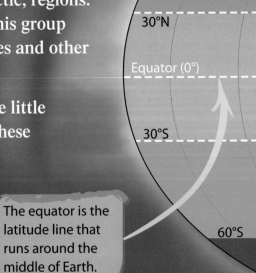

60°N

30°N

Equator (0°)

30°S

60°S

The equator is the latitude line that runs around the middle of Earth.

Changes in Latitude

Imaginary lines run around Earth north and south of the equator. These are *latitude lines*.

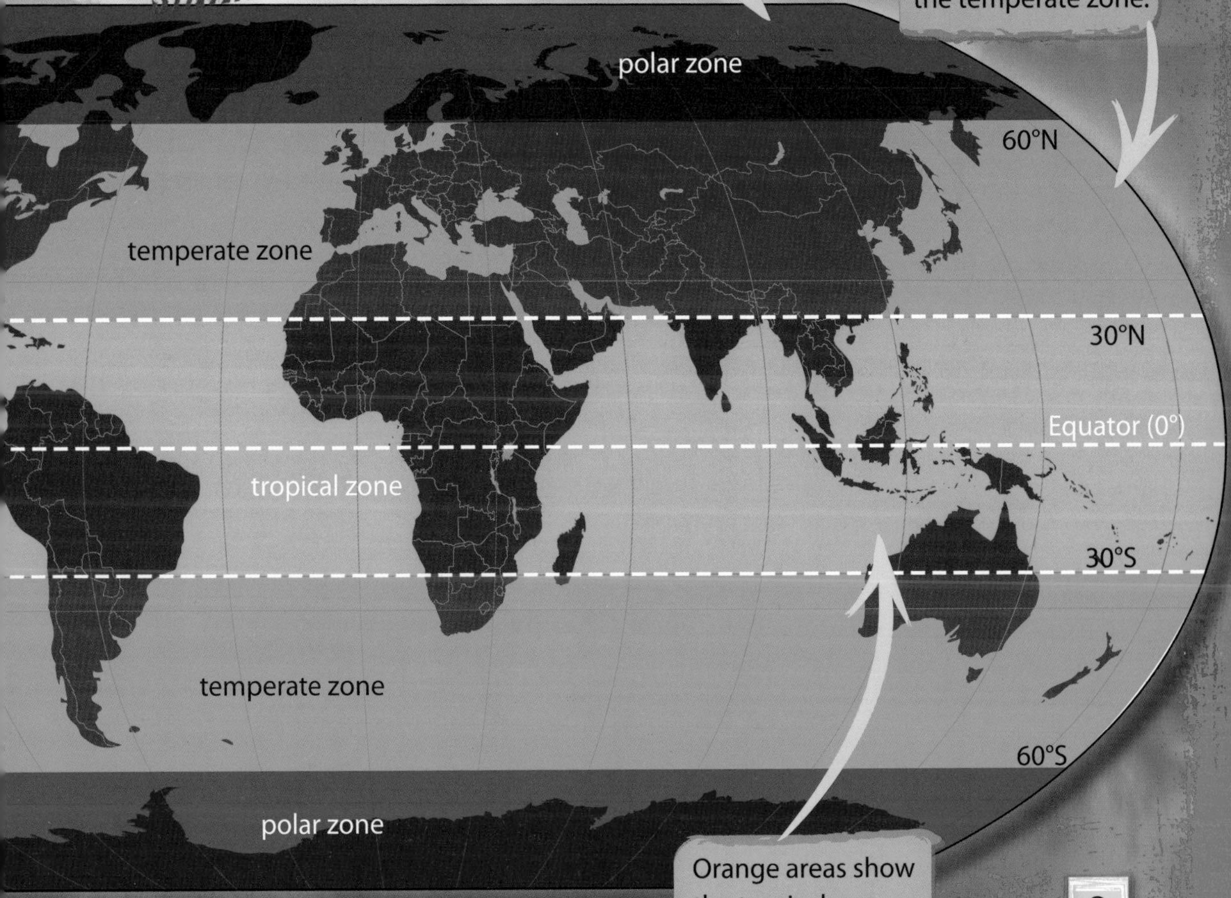

Purple areas show the polar zone.

Green areas show the temperate zone.

polar zone

60°N

temperate zone

30°N

Equator (0°)

tropical zone

30°S

temperate zone

60°S

polar zone

Orange areas show the tropical zone.

Low-Latitude Climates

Areas near the equator are famous for their warm, sunny climates. Many people love to vacation in these places.

Tropical Rainforests

Tropical rainforests are near the equator. There aren't any seasons in these areas. There is a lot of sunlight and warm temperatures all year. It is also **humid** year-round. This means there is a lot of moisture in the air. And, it rains all the time in the rainforest.

This warm wet climate is the perfect environment for plants to grow. There are many different types of plants in the rainforests, such as ferns and mosses. And there are huge trees! The highest layers of branches on these trees form a **canopy**. It acts like a roof for the rainforest. Millions of bugs and animals live under this roof. There are more types of living things in this climate than any other place on Earth. Colorful birds fly through the trees. Snakes slither around the floor. Monkeys swing from branches. And, frogs leap from place to place. You may even see a jaguar or a kinkajou (KING-kuh-joo).

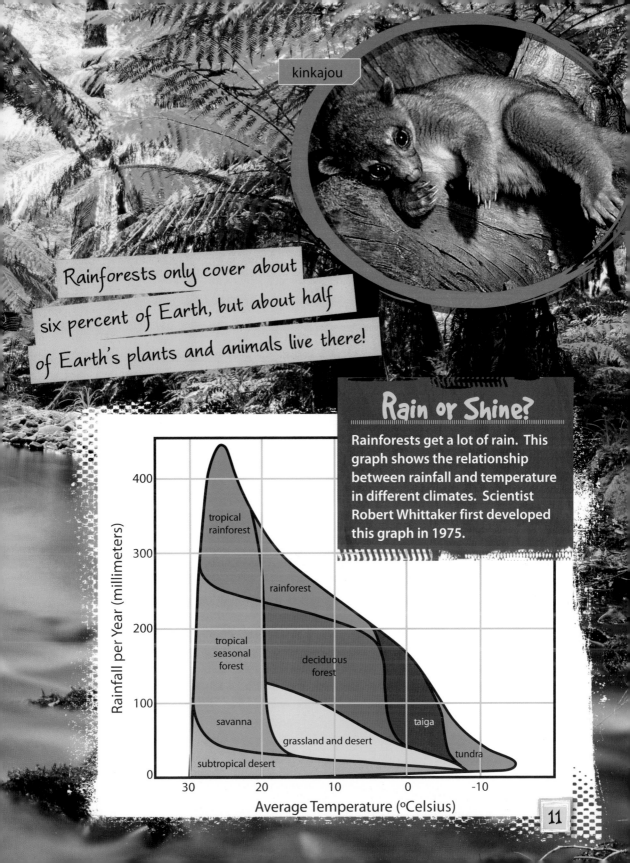

kinkajou

Rainforests only cover about six percent of Earth, but about half of Earth's plants and animals live there!

Rain or Shine?

Rainforests get a lot of rain. This graph shows the relationship between rainfall and temperature in different climates. Scientist Robert Whittaker first developed this graph in 1975.

Rainfall per Year (millimeters)

400

300

200

100

0

tropical rainforest

rainforest

tropical seasonal forest

deciduous forest

savanna

grassland and desert

taiga

tundra

subtropical desert

30   20   10   0   -10

Average Temperature (°Celsius)

Savannas

Have you ever seen photos from an African safari? There are elephants and zebras roaming the land. Sometimes, there is a fearless lion in a tree. Or maybe a giraffe is drinking water from a pond. But, have you ever noticed the land in the photos?

Grass feeds nearly all the animals that live in the savanna.

Savannas are found between rainforests and deserts. They are large flat areas of land. Savannas are covered with grass and a few scattered trees. In this climate, there is a wet summer season during which it rains a lot for a few months. Then, there is a longer dry winter season. During this time, there is little rainfall. There are also many lightning storms during winter. The lightning often strikes the ground. When this happens, the grass catches on fire. Large wildfires can spread quickly across the savanna. Although there is both winter and summer, the weather is warm year round.

Our Original Home

The first humans lived in the African savanna. Our ancestors thrived there. Even today, many people find this landscape calming. It is easy to see if someone is coming. There is plenty to eat. And the sunsets are beautiful.

Deserts

It's unusually hot in most desert climates. In fact, the ground gets so hot that it heats the air. You can actually see the air rise in waves. These waves can play tricks on your eyes. These are called *mirages* (mi-RAHZHs). They make people see things that are not really there. But, there is more to deserts than just high temperatures.

Many deserts are sandy and **barren**. Very few plants grow there. This is because deserts are arid, or dry. During the winter months, deserts get very little rain. Sometimes, it's so hot that the rain **evaporates**. The rainwater turns into a vapor, or gas, before it ever reaches the ground. This leaves hardly any water for plants and animals. At night, it gets cold in the desert. The temperature drops fast! This is because there is not a lot of moisture in the air. The desert climate is extreme, but life has **adapted**. Plants, animals, and humans all live in the desert.

rock hyrax

Useful Urine

Hyraxes (HAHY-ruh-seez) live in Africa and Asia. They prefer to urinate in the same places. Scientists found a place where the hyraxes had been urinating for 55,000 years! Over time, pollen, leaves, and grasses dried in the urine. Scientists studied how these plant bits changed over time. Their work showed how changes in the polar climates affected the climate in distant places such as Africa.

This loess plateau is used for farming in China.

Watching the Winds

When dust is blown for millions of years, it leaves behind loess (LOH-es). Scientists study loess to understand how winds blew in the past.

Mid-Latitude Climates

Areas farther from the equator are milder. These are popular places for plants and animals—including humans—to live.

African governments have created national parks to preserve Africa's beautiful grasslands.

Which Is Which?

Grasslands are very similar to savannas. So how can you tell the difference? Grasslands tend to have fewer trees—and more grass!

Grasslands

Grasslands are large, flat areas of land that are covered in different types of grasses. These areas do not receive enough rain for tall plants, such as trees, to grow. If they received less rain, it would be a desert climate. More rain would turn a grassland into a forest. This climate has cold winters and warm summers.

Most of the soil found in grasslands is rich. This means it is good for farming. Grasslands supply such staples as wheat and other grains. Grasslands are also perfect for growing corn.

Grazing animals love to eat all the types of grass. Grass is easy for them to reach. Plus, the grass grows back quickly after it is eaten. Bison (BAHY-suhn) and antelope can be seen grazing in grasslands. Farmers will often raise sheep and cattle on grassy land.

Change Is in the Wind

Without trees to break the wind, grasslands can become very windy places. If the soil becomes too dry, it can blow away. Over time, this can turn a grassland into a desert.

Mediterranean

The Mediterranean climate is an interesting one. It's a mild climate. It has four seasons, but it is often difficult to tell them apart. Winters are cool and moist. There is minimal rainfall and even less snow and ice. Summers are warm and dry. Spring and fall are nothing more than a mixture of winter and summer. Sometimes, it is tough to tell which season it is in this climate.

The areas with this climate are often close to the ocean where there is fog. There is hardly any rain. So, many plants in this climate have hairy leaves that can collect moisture from the fog. Plants in this climate have adapted in other ways, too. In the dry season, there are fires. Some plants have seeds that stay hidden in the ground until a fire sweeps across the land. The heat from the fire will crack a seed. Then, a plant will grow.

Parts of Australia, Chile, California, South Africa, and areas near the Mediterranean Sea have Mediterranean climates.

Diving for Data

The condition of Earth's oceans affects the climate on land. Scientists use small robots called *Argo floats* to record what's happening in the water. There are more than 3,500 Argo Floats in the ocean today.

Deciduous Forests

In this climate, it is easy to tell which season it is. Deciduous (dih-SIJ-oo-uhs) forests experience four distinct seasons. To tell which season it is, simply look at the leaves on the trees. Leaves change to beautiful colors in autumn. When winter comes, leaves fall off the trees. Then, they grow back in spring. Leaves are green during the summer season. This cycle helps trees stay alive during cold winter months. These trees include elm, oak, and maple.

Animals have to survive cold winter months, too. Some, such as the black bear, do this by hibernating. This means they spend the winter sleeping and resting. Other animals migrate. This means they temporarily move to warmer climates. While the winters are cold, summers are not too hot. And, this climate gets the most rain of any climate except, of course, the rainforest. It rains on and off throughout the year.

This black bear can hibernate in its warm den for up to seven months without food.

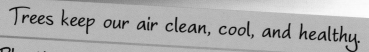

Trees keep our air clean, cool, and healthy.
Planting just one tree can help clean the air around you.

Revealing Rings

Every year, a tree grows a new ring in its trunk. The rings may be thinner or thicker depending on temperature, rainfall, and other factors. These rings can reveal important changes in the climate.

first-year growth

rainy season

dry season

scar from forest fire

High-Latitude Climates

Areas at the extreme ends of the planet have very cold climates. Scientists often study climate change in these areas. They track how quickly ice melts and where plants grow. Arctic areas are changing quickly. And these changes affect places around the world in big ways.

Watch Your Step

Muskegs form in places where permafrost and rock prevent water from draining from the soil. Moss, grasses, and trees may grow in these areas. That can make them look like solid ground. But the ground is actually wet and soft like a sponge.

Taiga Forests

This climate is very cold. Taiga (TAHY-guh) forests have summers that are short and cool. The wind blows down from the Arctic. So, the winters are long and very, very cold. Some parts of this climate are humid, while other areas experience very little rain. Most of the rain occurs during the short summers. There is, however, a lot of snow. In fact, a layer of soil beneath the forests in this climate is permanently frozen. That means it stays frozen. It is called *permafrost*.

Forests that grow in this cold climate are very thick. The trees include spruce, pine, and fir. These trees have needles for leaves. They are filled with sap. Sap is a watery juice inside a plant. It helps keep trees from freezing during long, cold winters. These trees are dark green. This helps them absorb sunlight.

Fierce Cold, Fierce Animals

Different types of animals can survive taiga forests. The most common are bears and moose. Birds live in this climate, but most of them migrate south for the winter. In Siberia, tigers roam the land!

Tundra

If you think taiga forests are cold, you should try living in the tundra! This is the area in the Arctic Circle that surrounds the North Pole. The climate is extremely cold there. Winters are long and dark. For several months, there is no sunlight. There is a very short mild season, but no real summer. During this mild season, the sun is out for 24 hours a day! There are no trees in this region due to the extreme cold. The region mostly consists of bare ground and rock. But, there is some plant life, such as moss and small shrubs.

You may think that there are no animals in this cold environment, but there are! There are caribou and arctic hares. There are foxes and wolves. There are even animals that live in chilly waters, such as walruses, beluga whales, and seals. And, there are polar bears! They are the most dangerous animals in this region.

beluga whales

Penguin Poop

When scientists learned that some penguins only nest on rocks, not ice, they had an idea. They worked their way across Antarctica, digging through bones, feathers, and dirt to find ancient penguin poop. The scientists recorded where each piece was found. They think these areas were rocky in the past. Their research shows that the climate has changed in Antarctica over the last 45,000 years.

penguin nesting place

Some pieces of penguin poop were 45,000 years old!

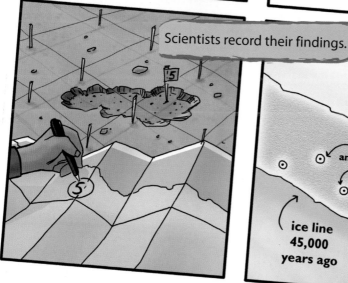

Scientists record their findings.

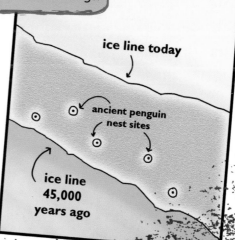

ice line today

ancient penguin nest sites

ice line 45,000 years ago

Climate Change

There are many different climates in our world. Some are cold, and others are hot. Some get lots of rain, and others get hardly any. Each climate has its own unique characteristics.

Today, scientists are observing changes in Earth's climate and temperature as a whole. They have noticed that it is getting warmer. The overall temperature on Earth is rising faster than normal. Most scientists think human behavior has caused this and other extreme changes. Grasslands are turning into deserts. And tundras are melting. Many places are experiencing intense storms and longer dry periods. Climate change is producing less snow on the ground and less ice in the oceans. The oceans are even rising.

Scientists around the world are collecting more data. They want to study the causes of climate change so they can slow it down. Together, they are finding ways to protect climates that are home to plants, animals, and humans all over the world.

"Knowledge empowers people with our most powerful tool: the ability to think and decide."

—Seymour Simon, writer

An Arctic glacier melts from the unusually warm weather.

Think Like a Scientist

How do clouds form? Experiment and find out!

What to Get

- food coloring
- hot water
- ice cubes
- large, clear jar
- small plate
- stopwatch

What to Do

1 Ask an adult to heat some water and pour it into the jar.

2 Add a drop of food coloring to the water.

3 Cover the jar with the plate. Let the jar sit for a minute. Look in the jar. What do you see?

4 Place ice cubes on the plate. Observe for a minute or two. What do you see?

Glossary

adapted—changed so that it is easier to live in a particular place

barren—having very few plants

canopy—the highest layer of branches in a forest

data—information used to calculate, analyze, or plan something

equator—an imaginary circle around the middle of Earth that is the same distance from the North Pole and the South Pole

evaporates—changes from a liquid into a gas

grazing—having the tendency to feed on small portions of plants throughout the day

humid—having a lot of moisture in the air

mild—not harsh

moisture—a small amount of liquid that makes things wet

Index

Your Turn!

Create a Climate

What climate do you live in? How do you know?
If you could create your ideal climate, what would it
be? What would the weather be like? What plants and
animals would live there? Draw a picture of your climate.